GENEVA TRAVEL GUIDE 2023

The Ultimate Geneva Travel Guide: Discover Top Attractions and Hidden Gems in this Breathtaking City of Peace For First Timers.

ANDREW NICHOLAS

Table of Contents

Introduction

Welcome to Geneva, the land of peace and serenity. Nestled in the heart of Europe, this charming Swiss city is a perfect blend of rich history, breathtaking landscapes, and world-class attractions. Whether you're a first-time visitor or a seasoned traveler, Geneva promises to captivate you with its unique blend of culture, history, and natural beauty. In this ultimate Geneva travel guide, we'll explore the top attractions and hidden gems that make Geneva a must-visit destination in 2023.

My Trip to Geneva, Switzerland

It was a crisp autumn morning when I set out on my journey to Geneva, the city of peace. I had heard so much about this picturesque city and was eager to explore its historic landmarks, world-class museums, and serene lakeside views.

As I landed at Geneva airport, I was greeted by the stunning beauty of the surrounding snow-capped Alps. After collecting my luggage, I hopped on a train to the city center and made my way to my hotel, which was located in the heart of Old Town. As I walked through the winding streets, I marveled at the charming architecture and the colorful buildings. When I arrived at my hotel, I was welcomed by the friendly staff, who gave me a map of the city and some recommendations for places to visit.

I started my trip by visiting the iconic Jet d'Eau fountain, one of the most recognizable landmarks in Geneva. The sight of the water jetting up into the sky was mesmerizing, and I spent a good amount of time taking photos and admiring the view.

After taking some photos, I made my way to the Parc des Bastions, where I saw the famous Reformation Wall and played a game of giant chess with some locals.

As the sun began to set, I made my way towards the shores of Lake Geneva. The shimmering blue waters and stunning views of the Alps took my breath away. I strolled along the promenade, enjoying the cool breeze and taking in the beauty of the city.

Then, I went to Carouge neighborhood, which is known for its vibrant nightlife and charming squares. I stopped at a cozy restaurant and had some traditional Swiss fondue, which was delicious. After dinner, I visited a jazz bar and listened to some local musicians play their hearts out.

On the second day of my trip, I visited the Palace of Nations, the headquarters of the United Nations in Europe. The guided tour provided fascinating insights into the workings of the international organization and its role in promoting peace and cooperation.

In the afternoon, I explored the Museum of Art and History, which housed an impressive collection of art and artifacts from different cultures and periods. I was particularly drawn to the ancient Egyptian section, with its impressive mummies and elaborate tombs.

On my last day in Geneva, I visited the St. Pierre Cathedral, which is a stunning example of Gothic architecture. I climbed to the top of the tower and was rewarded with a breathtaking view of the city and the Alps in the distance.

My trip to Geneva was a once-in-a-lifetime experience. I fell in love with the city's charm, beauty, and culture, and I know that I will come back someday. As I boarded my flight back home, I felt grateful for the memories I had made and the friends I had met along the way.

About Geneva

Geneva is a city in Switzerland, located at the southern tip of Lake Geneva, and is the second-largest city in the country. Known as the "Capital of Peace," Geneva is home to several international organizations, including the United Nations, the Red Cross, and the World Health Organization. This vibrant city is known for its rich cultural heritage, exquisite cuisine, and stunning architecture, making it one of the most popular tourist destinations in Switzerland.

Why Visit Geneva in 2023?

There are many reasons why you should consider visiting Geneva in 2023. Here are some of the top reasons:

Natural Beauty: Geneva is surrounded by breathtaking natural beauty, including the majestic Swiss Alps, crystal-clear Lake Geneva, and lush green parks. The city is also home to the famous Jet d'Eau, a stunning fountain that shoots water over 450 feet into the air.

Rich History: Geneva has a rich and fascinating history that dates back over 2,000 years. The city is home to several historic landmarks and museums, including the Old Town, St. Pierre Cathedral, and the International Museum of the Red Cross.

World-Class Attractions: Geneva is home to several world-class attractions, including the Palace of Nations, the United Nations headquarters in Europe, and the CERN, the European Organization for Nuclear Research, where the world's largest particle accelerator is located.

Luxury Shopping: Geneva is a city that is known for its luxury shopping. The city has several high-end boutiques and luxury stores, including Cartier, Chanel, and Louis Vuitton.

Cultural Events: Geneva hosts several cultural events throughout the year, including the Geneva International Film Festival, the Geneva Music Festival, and the Geneva International Motor Show.

Cuisine: Geneva is known for its exquisite cuisine, which is a unique blend of French and Swiss influences. The city is home to several Michelin-starred restaurants and local delicacies, such as fondue and raclette.

Best Time to Visit Geneva

The best time to visit Geneva is from mid-April to mid-October. During this time, the weather is mild, and the city is vibrant with plenty of outdoor activities, events, and festivals taking place.

The summer months of June to August are the peak tourist season, and the city is bustling with visitors. The streets are lined with musicians, performers, and vendors, creating a lively atmosphere, so expect larger crowds and higher prices.

However, if you want to avoid the crowds, it's best to visit during the shoulder seasons of March to May or September to November when the weather is still pleasant, and the crowds are thinner.

The winter months of December to March in Geneva can be harsh, but it's also a magical time to visit. The city is covered in snow, and you can experience the traditional Swiss Christmas markets and ski resorts. If you're planning to visit during the winter, make sure to pack warm clothing and prepare for possible flight delays due to snowstorms.

What to Take with You

Geneva is a cosmopolitan city, and you can find almost everything you need there. However, there are a few things you should take with you to make your stay more comfortable.

Comfortable Shoes: Geneva is a walking city, and you'll be doing a lot of it. Make sure you pack comfortable shoes to explore the city's many attractions.

Warm Clothes: If you're visiting in the winter months, make sure you pack warm clothes, including a winter coat, gloves, and a hat. The temperatures can drop below freezing, and there's a chance of snow.

Swiss Francs: Although most places in Geneva accept credit cards, it's always handy to have some Swiss francs with you for smaller purchases, like a coffee or a croissant from a local bakery.

Rain Gear: Geneva is known for its unpredictable weather, so pack a rain jacket and umbrella to stay dry in case of sudden showers.

Travel Adapter: Switzerland has a different electrical system than most countries, and you'll need a travel adapter to charge your electronic devices.

Sunscreen: If you're visiting during the summer months, make sure you pack sunscreen to protect yourself from the strong sun rays.

Camera: Geneva is a beautiful city with many photo opportunities, so don't forget to pack your camera to capture all the memorable moments.

Chapter 1

Top Tourist Attractions In Geneva

If you're planning to visit Geneva, Switzerland in 2023, you are in for a treat! The "City of Peace" is a wonderful destination for first-time visitors. It's a hub of international diplomacy and home to many famous landmarks. Here's a guide to the top tourist attractions in Geneva that you should definitely include in your itinerary.

Jet d'Eau

The Jet d'Eau is one of Geneva's most iconic landmarks and a must-see for any first-time visitor. The fountain shoots water up to 140 meters into the air, creating a magnificent spectacle that can be seen from miles away. You can get up close to the Jet d'Eau by taking a boat tour on Lake Geneva, or you can simply stroll along the Quai du Mont-Blanc for a closer look.

St. Pierre Cathedral

The St. Pierre Cathedral is a stunning gothic cathedral located in the heart of Geneva's Old Town. The cathedral dates back to the 12th century and features intricate stained glass windows and impressive architecture. Visitors can climb the stairs to the top of the cathedral's towers for breathtaking views of the city and the surrounding mountains.

Old Town Geneva

Old Town Geneva is a charming neighborhood with cobblestone streets, historic buildings, and quaint shops and cafes. Visitors can take a stroll through the old town and explore its many attractions, such as the Maison Tavel Museum, the Reformation Wall, and the Place du Bourg-de-Four.

Palais des Nations

The Palais des Nations is the European headquarters of the United Nations and is one of the most significant international conference centers in the world. Visitors can take a guided tour of the building and learn about the UN's history and current initiatives.

United Nations Office at Geneva

The United Nations Office at Geneva is another important international organization that has its headquarters in Geneva. Visitors can take a guided tour of the building and learn about the UN's work in areas such as human rights, disarmament, and sustainable development.

Reformation Wall

The Reformation Wall is a monument in Geneva that commemorates the Protestant Reformation. The monument features statues of prominent figures such as John Calvin and William Farel, who played important roles in the Reformation movement.

CERN

CERN (European Organization for Nuclear Research) is located just outside of Geneva and is the world's largest particle physics laboratory.

Chapter 2

Best Transportation Options

Geneva is a popular destination for tourists from all over the world, it is no wonder that many visitors come to this city every year. Geneva is a compact city and getting around is easy thanks to the well-developed public transportation system. To make your trip as smooth and comfortable as possible, it is important to know the best transport options to get to and around the city.

Getting to Geneva

By Air: Geneva International Airport (GVA) is the main airport serving the city. It is located just 4 km from the city center and has excellent transport links to the city.

The airport serves many international airlines, including Swiss International Air Lines, easyJet, British Airways, and Lufthansa, among others.

By Train: Geneva is well-connected to many major cities in Europe by train. The city has two major train stations: Geneva Cornavin and Geneva Eaux-Vives. Both stations are located in the city center and have frequent trains to major European cities such as Paris, Milan, and Barcelona.

By Bus: There are several bus companies that operate from Geneva to many European cities. Flixbus is a popular bus company that offers affordable and comfortable bus services to several destinations in Europe.

By Car: If you are planning to drive to Geneva, it is important to note that the city has several paid parking areas. Also, traffic can be quite busy during peak hours, so it is important to plan your route in advance.

Getting Around Geneva

Public Transportation: Geneva has an excellent public transportation system consisting of buses, trams, and trains. The network is run by the Geneva Public Transport (TPG) company, and tickets can be purchased at ticket machines or online. The system is reliable, affordable, and covers most parts of the city.

Taxis: Taxis are widely available in Geneva, but they can be quite expensive. It is recommended to book a taxi in advance or use a ride-hailing service like Uber or Lyft.

Bicycles: Geneva is a bike-friendly city with many dedicated bike lanes and bike-sharing services. The city has a bike-sharing program called "Genève Roule," which allows visitors to rent a bike for a small fee.

Walking: Geneva is a compact city, and many of the top attractions are within walking distance of each other. Walking is an excellent way to explore the city, and it is free!

Boats: Geneva is located on the shores of Lake Geneva, and boat tours are a popular way to see the city from a different perspective. Many boat tours operate from the city center and offer stunning views of the surrounding mountains and the lake.

Chapter 3

Best Accommodation Guide

When it comes to finding the perfect place to stay in Geneva, there are plenty of options to choose from. Whether you're looking for a luxury hotel, a budget-friendly hostel, or something in between, Geneva has it all. In this chapter, we'll explore the different types of accommodations available in Geneva and provide some tips on where to stay in this beautiful city.

Types of Accommodations

1. Hotels: Geneva is home to a range of hotels, from luxurious five-star hotels to more affordable options. The city has a variety of hotels that cater to different budgets and needs. Some popular hotels in Geneva include the Hotel d'Angleterre, the Mandarin Oriental Geneva, and the Grand Hotel Kempinski Geneva.

2. Hostels: If you're looking for a more affordable option, hostels are a great choice. Geneva has several hostels that offer clean and comfortable accommodations at a reasonable price. Some popular hostels in Geneva include the City Hostel Geneva, the Geneva Hostel, and the Youth Hostel Geneva.

3. Apartments: Renting an apartment is a great option for travelers who want to experience Geneva like a local. There are several websites where you can rent apartments in Geneva for short-term stays. This option is ideal for families or groups of friends who want to have their own space.

4. Bed and Breakfasts: Bed and breakfasts are a great option for travelers who want a more personal experience. In Geneva, there are several bed and breakfasts that offer comfortable accommodations and a home-like atmosphere. Some popular bed and breakfasts in Geneva include the Villa Esprit3 and the B&B Qu'Importe.

Where to Stay in Geneva

Old Town: If you want to experience the charm and history of Geneva, Old Town is the place to be. This area is filled with narrow streets, charming cafes, and historical landmarks. Some popular hotels in Old Town include the Hotel Les Armures and the Hotel de la Cigogne.

Lake Geneva: For those who want to enjoy the beautiful views of Lake Geneva, staying near the lake is a great choice. This area is home to some of the most luxurious hotels in Geneva, such as the Hotel President Wilson and the Beau-Rivage Geneva.

Carouge: For a more local experience, consider staying in Carouge. This bohemian neighborhood is known for its vibrant nightlife, charming squares, and colorful buildings. Staying in Carouge will give you easy access to the city's top museums, like the Museum of Modern and Contemporary Art.

Paquis: If you're looking for a lively and vibrant neighborhood, Paquis is the place to be. This area is known for its trendy bars and restaurants, as well as its proximity to the lake. Some popular hotels in Paquis include the Hotel N'vY and the Warwick Geneva.

Plainpalais: For those who want to be in the heart of the action, Plainpalais is a great choice. This area is home to the University of Geneva and is known for its lively nightlife and cultural attractions. Some popular hotels in Plainpalais include the Hotel Tiffany and the Hotel Bristol.

Chapter 4

Hidden Gems and Off-the-Beaten-Path Destinations

Geneva is a city that is full of hidden gems and off-the-beaten-path destinations waiting to be discovered. From historic buildings to picturesque parks, Geneva has it all. Here are some of the top hidden gems and off-the-beaten-path destinations that you should not miss on your visit to this breathtaking city of peace:

1. **Carouge**

Carouge is a quaint neighborhood in Geneva that's often compared to Italy's Piedmont region due to its Italianate architecture and laid-back vibe. This charming area is located just a few kilometers south of the city center and is an excellent place to escape the crowds and soak up the local culture. Stroll along the cobblestone streets and marvel at the beautiful pastel-colored buildings that house cafes, artisan shops, and independent boutiques. The Place du Marché is the central square of Carouge, where you can enjoy a coffee or an aperitif and watch the world go by.

If you're a foodie, Carouge won't disappoint you. This neighborhood is known for its gourmet food scene, and there are several excellent restaurants where you can indulge in traditional Swiss cuisine and international dishes.

2. Bains des Pâquis

Bains des Pâquis is a hidden gem located on a small peninsula on the shores of Lake Geneva. It's a local favorite, and it's not uncommon to see people swimming, sunbathing, and having picnics here. The Bains des Pâquis complex includes a restaurant, sauna, Turkish bath, and a range of wellness services. In the winter, you can even take a dip in the lake's icy waters as part of the traditional Swiss New Year's Day celebration.

If you're visiting in the evening, head to the restaurant and enjoy a fondue or raclette while taking in the spectacular views of the lake and the Jet d'Eau.

3. Villa Diodati

Literature buffs should not miss a visit to Villa Diodati, which has a fascinating history. This historic mansion located on the shores of Lake Geneva was where Lord Byron, Percy Bysshe Shelley, and Mary Shelley spent a summer in 1816. It was during this time that Mary Shelley wrote Frankenstein, which is widely regarded as one of the greatest horror novels ever written.

The villa has since been restored and is now a private residence, but visitors can still admire its beautiful architecture and explore the surrounding gardens. There's also a plaque outside the villa that commemorates the famous literary figures who once stayed here.

4. **Plainpalais Flea Market**

If you're a fan of vintage or secondhand goods, you'll love the Plainpalais Flea Market. This popular market takes place every Wednesday and Saturday and is the perfect place to hunt for unique treasures.

Here, you'll find everything from vintage clothing and accessories to furniture, artwork, and antiques. It's also a great place to sample some local food and soak up the lively atmosphere.

5. **Gardens of Geneva's Conservatory and Botanical**

One of the city's hidden gems is the Conservatory and Botanical Garden of the City of Geneva. Over 16,000 different plant species, many of which are rare and endangered, can be found in this stunning garden. Additionally, there is a butterfly house and a greenhouse in the garden filled with tropical plants. The lovely flowers and plants can be admired by visitors when they wander gently through the garden. In addition to the garden, there is a museum there featuring displays on environmental history and plant life.

6. Parc des Bastions

Parc des Bastions is a hidden gem located in the Old Town of Geneva. This beautiful park features a chessboard with giant pieces that people can play with, a statue of Jean-Jacques Rousseau, and beautiful landscaping. The park is a great place to relax and take a break from the hustle and bustle of the city. It also has a playground for children, making it a great spot for families.

7. Quartier des Grottes

The Quartier des Grottes is a charming neighborhood located just a few minutes' walk from the city center. The area is known for its unique architecture, which includes a number of old-fashioned houses and buildings with colorful facades. One of the highlights of the Quartier des Grottes is the Passage des Lions, a narrow alleyway that is home to a number of art galleries and studios.

Visitors can wander through the alleyway, admiring the artwork on display and chatting with the artists themselves. This neighborhood is also home to a number of trendy bars and cafes, making it a great place to grab a drink or a bite to eat. The Quartier des Grottes is a hidden gem that is well worth a visit.

8. The Viaduct

The Viaduct is a unique shopping destination that is located in the district of Plainpalais. The shopping center is housed in an old railway viaduct and features a variety of independent shops and boutiques selling everything from fashion and accessories to home decor and gourmet foods.

In addition to the shops, the Viaduct is also home to several cafes and restaurants, making it a great place to grab a bite to eat or a cup of coffee. The center is open year-round and admission is free.

9. Victoria Hall

Victoria Hall is a stunning concert hall located in the heart of Geneva. The hall was built in 1891 and is known for its excellent acoustics and beautiful interior. The hall hosts a variety of concerts throughout the year, ranging from classical music to jazz and world music.

Visitors can take a guided tour of the hall to learn more about its history and architecture. The tour includes a visit to the stage, backstage area, and dressing rooms

Chapter 5

Culinary Delights, Regional Specialties and Restaurants

Geneva is known not only for its stunning scenery and rich culture but also for its culinary delights. When it comes to dining in Geneva, the city offers a wide range of culinary delights, from traditional Swiss cuisine to international dishes. The city boasts an impressive range of dining options, from high-end restaurants to local eateries that serve traditional Swiss dishes. Here are some of the best restaurants and bars to try during your visit to Geneva.

Traditional Swiss Dishes

Fondue - This dish consists of melted cheese served in a communal pot, along with bread cubes for dipping. It's a classic Swiss dish that's perfect for sharing with friends.

Raclette - This is another cheesy dish that's similar to fondue but is typically served with boiled potatoes, pickled onions, and cured meats.

Rosti - This dish consists of grated potatoes that are fried until crispy and golden brown. It's typically served as a side dish with meat or eggs.

Zurcher Geschnetzeltes - This dish is a creamy veal stew served with rosti or noodles.

Birchermuesli - A healthy and delicious breakfast dish made with oats, nuts, fruit, and yogurt.

Chocolate - While not a dish, Switzerland is famous for its high-quality chocolate. Be sure to try some of the local chocolate while in Geneva.

These dishes can be found in most Swiss restaurants in Geneva. However, if you're looking for an authentic Swiss dining experience, head to Les Armures, a historic restaurant in Old Town Geneva that offers traditional Swiss cuisine in a charming atmosphere.

Chocolate and Pastry Shops

Auer Chocolatier - This chocolate shop has been around since 1939 and is known for its handmade truffles, pralines, and chocolate bars.

Favarger - This is the oldest chocolate factory in Geneva, dating back to 1826. They produce high-quality chocolates and ice cream.

Patisserie Chatillon - This pastry shop is known for its macarons, cakes, and tarts. They use only the best ingredients, and their creations are as beautiful as they are delicious.

Du Rhône Chocolatier - Another famous chocolatier, Du Rhône offers a wide range of handmade chocolates and pastries. The shop's specialties include truffles, pralines, and macarons.

La Chocolaterie de Genève - This chocolate shop offers a unique twist to traditional Swiss chocolates. They specialize in creating chocolates with unexpected flavors, such as saffron, ginger, and jasmine.

Wine Tasting

Geneva is known for its wine, particularly its white wine made from the Chasselas grape. Here are a few places to try some local wines:

Caves Ouvertes - This annual event in May allows visitors to explore the vineyards and wineries of the Canton of Geneva. You can sample wines, meet winemakers, and learn about the winemaking process.

Domaine Les Perrières - This winery is located in the heart of the vineyards of Satigny, just a short drive from Geneva. They offer guided tours and wine tastings, where you can sample their delicious Chasselas, Pinot Noir, and Gamay wines.

Cave de Genève - This winery, located just a few minutes from the city center, offers a wide range of wines from the Geneva region. They offer guided tours and tastings, where you can sample some of their award-winning wines.

Best Restaurants in Geneva

La Bottega: La Bottega is a traditional Italian restaurant located in the heart of Geneva's old town. The restaurant offers a rustic atmosphere and a menu that features fresh homemade pasta, wood-fired pizzas, and traditional Italian specialties.

Les Armures: Les Armures is a historic restaurant that dates back to the 17th century. It is located in the heart of Geneva's old town and features traditional Swiss cuisine. The menu includes fondue, raclette, and other local dishes.

Auberge de Savièse: Auberge de Savièse is a charming Swiss restaurant that is popular with locals and tourists alike. The menu features traditional Swiss dishes such as rösti, cheese fondue, and sausages.

Chez Philippe - This restaurant is located in the heart of the city and is known for its impeccable service and classic French cuisine. The menu features dishes like escargot, foie gras, and lamb chops. The elegant atmosphere and attention to detail make Chez Philippe a favorite among locals and tourists alike.

Izumi: Izumi is a Japanese restaurant located in the trendy Eaux-Vives neighborhood. The menu includes sushi, sashimi, and other Japanese specialties.

Bayview by Michel Roth: Another Michelin-starred restaurant, Bayview by Michel Roth is located on the eighth floor of the Hotel President Wilson and offers panoramic views of the lake and the city. The menu features creative French cuisine with a focus on seafood.

Café du Soleil: Café du Soleil is a cozy bistro located in the Carouge neighborhood. The menu features traditional Swiss cuisine such as rosti and fondue, as well as French-inspired dishes.

Bars and Pubs in Geneva

Mr. Pickwick Pub: Mr. Pickwick Pub is a traditional English pub located in the heart of Geneva's old town. The pub offers a wide selection of beers, including English ales and Belgian beers.

L'Atelier Cocktail Club: L'Atelier Cocktail Club is a trendy cocktail bar located in the city center. The bar offers an extensive cocktail menu and a lively atmosphere.

Bottle Brothers: Bottle Brothers is a popular wine bar located in the Eaux-Vives neighborhood. The bar offers a selection of wines from around the world, as well as a small menu of snacks.

Les Brasseurs: Les Brasseurs is a microbrewery located in the Plainpalais neighborhood. The brewery offers a variety of craft beers, as well as traditional Swiss dishes.

La Clémence: La Clémence is a popular bar located in the Carouge neighborhood. The bar offers a wide selection of beers, wines, and cocktails, as well as live music on weekends.

Nightlife

Geneva's nightlife scene offers something for everyone, from lively clubs to cozy bars and jazz clubs. Here are some of the top nightlife spots in Geneva:

Le Chat Noir - This nightclub has a trendy and eclectic atmosphere, and is a popular spot for locals and tourists alike. The menu features classic cocktails, as well as unique creations like the "Smoky Old Fashioned." The bar also hosts live music performances on the weekends.

Java Club: Java Club is a popular nightclub located in the city center. The club features DJs playing a mix of electronic, hip-hop, and pop music.

Club Nautique: Club Nautique is a nightclub located on the shores of Lake Geneva. The club features a large dance floor and a terrace with stunning views of the lake.

Moulin Rouge: Moulin Rouge is a cabaret-style club located in the Eaux-Vives neighborhood. The club features live performances by dancers and singers.

Le Baroque: Le Baroque is a popular nightclub located in the Plainpalais neighborhood. The club features multiple dance floors, as well as a VIP area.

Brasserie des Halles de l'Ile - This restaurant and bar is located in a historic building on an island in the Rhone river. The bar has a lively atmosphere and serves a wide selection of beers and cocktails.

La Graviere - This club is located in an underground space and is known for its diverse music lineup, including reggae, hip-hop, and electronic music. The club also hosts cultural events like film screenings and art exhibitions.

Rooftop 42: Located on the 42nd floor of the Hotel President Wilson, Rooftop 42 offers stunning views of the lake and the city. The bar hosts regular events and DJ sets, making it a popular spot for nightlife in Geneva.

Chapter 6

Day Trips from Geneva

Geneva is a beautiful city with a lot to offer, but if you're looking to explore beyond its boundaries, there are plenty of exciting day trips you can take. Here are some top destinations worth visiting:

Annecy, France

Annecy is a charming town located just 40 kilometers from Geneva, on the edge of Lake Annecy. Known as the "Venice of the Alps," Annecy is famous for its picturesque canals, stunning scenery, and medieval architecture. You can take a stroll through the old town and admire the colorful houses, visit the stunning Chateau d'Annecy, or take a boat tour of the lake.

Lausanne, Switzerland

Located just 62 kilometers from Geneva, Lausanne is a vibrant city overlooking Lake Geneva. It is home to the International Olympic Committee and has a rich history and culture. You can visit the Olympic Museum, stroll through the charming old town, or explore the museums and galleries. The city also has some excellent restaurants and shops, as well as a lively nightlife.

Chamonix-Mont-Blanc, France

Chamonix is a famous ski resort located in the French Alps, just 88 kilometers from Geneva. It offers some of the most stunning views of Mont Blanc, the highest mountain in Europe. You can take the cable car up to Aiguille du Midi, which offers panoramic views of the mountains, or enjoy skiing or snowboarding in the winter. In the summer, you can go hiking, rock climbing, or paragliding.

Montreux

Located just 93 kilometers from Geneva, Montreux is a charming town on the shores of Lake Geneva. It is famous for its beautiful promenade, lined with palm trees and flowers, and the stunning Chateau de Chillon, a medieval castle that inspired Lord Byron's poem, "The Prisoner of Chillon." You can take a boat tour of the lake, visit the Freddie Mercury statue, or explore the jazz festival that takes place every year in July.

Gruyères

Located 110 kilometers from Geneva, Gruyères is a charming medieval town known for its famous cheese. You can visit the Gruyère cheese factory and learn how the cheese is made, stroll through the cobblestone streets of the old town, or visit the Gruyères Castle, which dates back to the 13th century. The town also offers stunning views of the surrounding mountains and is a great destination for nature lovers.

Chapter 7

Geneva's Art and Culture Scene

Geneva boasts of several art galleries, museums, and festivals that cater to the interests of art lovers and history buffs. Here is a detailed guide to Geneva's art and culture scene that you should not miss.

Art Galleries

If you are an art enthusiast, then Geneva's art galleries should definitely be on your list. There are several art galleries in the city that showcase contemporary and modern art pieces by local and international artists. The following are some of the popular art galleries in Geneva:

Galerie d'Art Contemporain - This art gallery is known for its modern and contemporary art pieces. It features works by renowned artists like Picasso, Warhol, and Matisse.

Artigny Gallery - One of the must-visit galleries in Geneva is the Artigny Gallery, which is housed in a stunning 19th-century mansion. This gallery features a diverse collection of art, including paintings, sculptures, and mixed media pieces.

Museum of Modern and Contemporary Art (MAMCO) - This museum is one of the best places to experience contemporary art in Geneva. It showcases works by local and international artists, including painting, sculpture, video, and installations.

Espace Muraille - This gallery is located in an old castle and features contemporary art pieces. It is a popular venue for exhibitions and events.

Museums

Geneva is home to several museums that showcase the city's rich history and culture. These museums offer a glimpse into the city's past, art, and technology. Here are some of the popular museums in Geneva:

Musée d'Histoire Naturelle - This museum is a must-visit for nature lovers. It features exhibits on the history of the earth, the animal kingdom, and the plant world. It also has a collection of over 12,000 specimens, including fossils, rocks, and minerals.

Patek Philippe Museum - This museum showcases the history of watchmaking in Geneva. It features over 2,000 timepieces, including some of the world's most expensive watches.

International Red Cross and Red Crescent Museum - This museum showcases the history and work of the International Red Cross and Red Crescent Movement. It features exhibits on the organization's humanitarian work around the world.

Centre d'Art Contemporain - If you're interested in modern and contemporary art, the Centre d'Art Contemporain is a must-visit museum. This museum showcases works of art from emerging and established artists, with a focus on contemporary art practices.

Festivals

Geneva is known for its vibrant festival scene. The city hosts several festivals throughout the year, celebrating art, music, food, and culture. Here are some of the popular festivals in Geneva:

Geneva International Film Festival - This festival is dedicated to showcasing independent films from around the world. It features screenings, workshops, and talks with filmmakers.

Geneva Music Festival - This festival celebrates music from various genres, including classical, jazz, and rock. It features concerts and performances by local and international artists.

Fêtes de Genève - This festival is one of the biggest events in the city. It features concerts, food stalls, and carnival rides. It takes place in August and attracts thousands of visitors every year.

Chapter 8

Outdoor Activities in Geneva

Lake Geneva Cruise: A must-do activity when in Geneva is taking a cruise on Lake Geneva. The lake is a stunning sight to see and is surrounded by snow-capped mountains. There are many different types of cruises available, ranging from short 1-hour sightseeing tours to full-day excursions that take you to various towns around the lake. During the cruise, you'll get to enjoy breathtaking views of the Swiss Alps, French Alps, and the famous Jet d'Eau, a stunning water fountain that shoots water 140 meters into the air. If you're lucky, you may even catch a glimpse of the majestic Mont Blanc, Europe's highest mountain.

Hiking in the Jura Mountains: If you're a nature lover, you'll love hiking in the Jura Mountains. Located just outside of Geneva, the Jura Mountains offer a network of hiking trails that cater to all levels of hikers. You'll get to explore dense forests, rolling hills, and stunning alpine meadows, all while enjoying breathtaking views of the surrounding mountains. During the summer months, you can also enjoy activities such as paragliding and mountain biking.

Jet Boat Rides: For those seeking a thrilling adventure, a jet boat ride on Lake Geneva is a must-do. These high-speed boats can reach speeds of up to 90 km/h and will take you on a wild ride across the lake. You'll get to experience adrenaline-pumping maneuvers such as

360-degree spins, power slides, and fish tails, all while taking in the stunning scenery around you. It's a great activity for families, groups of friends, or solo travelers looking for a unique experience.

Skiing and Snowboarding: During the winter months, skiing and snowboarding are some of the top outdoor activities in Geneva. There are several ski resorts located within an hour's drive from the city, including Les Portes du Soleil and Chamonix Mont-Blanc. These resorts offer a wide range of runs, catering to all levels of skiers and snowboarders. You can also enjoy other winter activities such as ice skating, snowshoeing, and sledding.

Parc des Bastions: If you're looking for a peaceful outdoor activity, head to Parc des Bastions. This beautiful park is located in the heart of Geneva and is home to the famous Reformation Wall, a tribute to the leaders of the Protestant Reformation. The park also features a large chess board where you can challenge other visitors to a game of chess or simply relax and enjoy the scenery.

Jardin Botanique: For those who love flowers and gardens, the Jardin Botanique is a must-visit attraction. This beautiful botanical garden features over 16,000 plant species from around the world. The garden covers over 28 hectares and is split into several sections, including an alpine garden, a rose garden, and a medicinal garden. There's also a greenhouse that houses tropical plants and a collection of cacti. The Jardin Botanique is a great place to learn about different plant species and enjoy a peaceful stroll.

Mont Salève: Mont Salève is a mountain that offers stunning views of Geneva and the surrounding area. You can reach the summit by taking a cable car from the nearby town of Veyrier. Once at the top, you can enjoy the views and even try paragliding if you're feeling adventurous. This is a great place to escape the city and enjoy some fresh mountain air.

Chapter 9

Practical Tips for Traveling in Geneva

To make the most out of your trip to Geneva, it is essential to consider some practical tips that will make your stay comfortable and enjoyable. In this chapter, we will discuss two crucial aspects of traveling in Geneva: budgeting for your trip and language and cultural etiquettes.

Budgeting for your trip

Before embarking on any trip, it is crucial to budget for it. Geneva is known for being an expensive city, so it is essential to plan accordingly to avoid overspending. Here are some tips for budgeting for your trip to Geneva:

1. **Plan ahead**: Research on the average costs of transportation, accommodation, food, and activities in Geneva. This will give you an idea of how much you need to save for your trip.

2. **Consider off-peak seasons**: Geneva can be quite expensive during peak seasons, such as summer and winter. Consider traveling during the shoulder seasons, such as spring and fall, to save on costs.

3. **Use public transportation**: Public transportation in Geneva is efficient and affordable. Consider using buses and trams instead of taxis, which can be quite expensive.

4. Look for budget-friendly accommodations: Geneva has a range of accommodation options, from luxurious hotels to budget-friendly hostels. Consider staying in a hostel or Airbnb to save on costs.

5. Food: Eating out in Geneva can be expensive, but there are ways to save money. Look for local markets and grocery stores to buy fresh produce and prepare your meals. Alternatively, look for affordable restaurants that offer set menus or daily specials.

6. Take advantage of free activities: Geneva has many free activities, such as walking tours, parks, and museums. Take advantage of these activities to save on costs.

Language and Cultural Etiquettes

Geneva is a multilingual city, with French, German, and English being the primary languages spoken. Here are some language and cultural etiquettes to keep in mind when traveling to Geneva:

1. **Greetings**: In Geneva, it is customary to greet people with a handshake. When meeting someone for the first time, say "bonjour" or "salut" in French.

2. **Language:** French is the most commonly spoken language in Geneva. However, many people also speak English and German, so it is helpful to learn some basic phrases in these languages.

3. Dress code: Geneva is a cosmopolitan city, and people generally dress smartly. When visiting religious sites, it is recommended to dress conservatively.

4. Tipping: Tipping is not mandatory in Geneva, but it is appreciated. A tip of 10% is considered generous.

5. Punctuality: Swiss people value punctuality, and it's essential to be on time for appointments and meetings. If you are running late, it's courteous to call and let the other person know.

6. Public behavior: Geneva is known for its peaceful and respectful culture. It is essential to be mindful of your behavior in public spaces and to respect the local culture and customs.

Useful phrases in Swiss German, French, Italian, and Romansh

It's an excellent idea to acquire a few fundamental phrases in the local languages even if many Swiss people speak English. The following are some useful expressions in Romansh, French, Italian, and Swiss German:

Swiss German

Guten Tag (Good day)

Grüezi (grew-tsi) - Hello (formal)

Hoi (hoy) - Hi (informal)

Danke (Thank you)

Bitte (Please)

Wie geht's? (vee gohts) - How are you?

Mir gönd guet (I'm fine)

S'isch mir en Fröid (It's my pleasure)

S'isch okay (It's okay)

En schöne Tag! (en shern-uh tahg) - Have a nice day!
Tschüss (Goodbye)

French

Bonjour (bohn-zhoor) - (Hello/Good day)
Merci (mehr-see) - (Thank you)
S'il vous plaît (Please)
Comment ça va? (kom-mohn sah vah) - (How are you?)
Ça va bien, merci (I'm fine, thank you)
De rien (You're welcome)
Excusez-moi (Excuse me)
Je ne parle pas français (I don't speak French)
Bonne journée (bohn jurn-ay) - Have a nice day!
Au revoir (oh ruh-vwahr) (Goodbye)

Italian

Buongiorno (Good day)

Grazie (Thank you)

Per favore (Please)

Come va? (How are you?)

Sto bene, grazie (I'm fine, thank you)

Prego (You're welcome)

Scusi (Excuse me)

Non parlo italiano (I don't speak Italian)

Arrivederci (Goodbye)

Romansh

Bun di (Hello/Good day)

Grazia (Thank you)

Per favore (Please)

Co vai? (How are you?)

Vua bien, grazia (I'm fine, thank you)

Cun plaschair (You're welcome)

Excusa (Excuse me)

Yo na parla rumantsch (I don't speak Romansh)

Adeus (Goodbye)

Safety and Security

Geneva is considered a safe city for tourists. However, it is always wise to take precautions to ensure your safety while traveling. Keep this tips in mind:

1. **Keep your valuables safe**: Keep your valuables such as passports, cash, and credit cards in a secure place. Do not leave them unattended in your hotel room or in public places. Always keep them close to you, preferably in a money belt or a secure bag.

2. **Be aware of your surroundings**: Be aware of your surroundings and keep an eye out for any suspicious activity. Avoid walking alone in poorly lit areas or deserted streets at night.

3. Follow traffic rules: In Geneva, traffic moves on the right-hand side of the road. Pedestrians should use marked crosswalks and obey traffic signals. It is illegal to jaywalk in Geneva.

4. Beware of pickpockets: Pickpockets operate in crowded tourist areas such as train stations, shopping malls, and markets. Be vigilant and keep your belongings close to you. Avoid carrying large sums of cash.

5. Be cautious of street vendors: While most street vendors in Geneva are legitimate, there are some who may try to scam tourists by selling fake products or overcharging for goods. If you do decide to buy from a street vendor, be sure to negotiate the price and check the quality of the product before purchasing.

6. Emergency numbers: In case of an emergency, dial 112 for police, ambulance, or fire department.

Shopping

Geneva is a shopper's paradise. The city offers a wide range of shopping options, from luxury boutiques to flea markets. Here are some shopping experience tips

Geneva's luxury shopping district: Geneva's luxury shopping district is located on Rue du Rhone. Here you will find high-end brands such as Chanel, Louis Vuitton, and Prada.

Markets: Geneva has several markets where you can find unique souvenirs and gifts. The Plainpalais Flea Market is held every Wednesday and Saturday, while the

Carouge Market takes place every Wednesday.

Swiss chocolates: Switzerland is famous for its chocolates, and Geneva has several chocolatiers that sell delicious Swiss chocolates. Some popular brands include Teuscher, Auer, and Favarger.

Swiss watches: Switzerland is also famous for its watches. Geneva has several watchmakers that offer a wide range of luxury watches. Some popular brands include Rolex, Patek Philippe, and Omega.

VAT refund: Non-EU tourists are entitled to a refund of the Value Added Tax (VAT) on goods they purchase in Geneva. To claim your refund, you must present your passport and a completed VAT refund form at the airport.

Tips for Traveling with Children

Plan Ahead: Research kid-friendly activities and attractions in Geneva before your trip. This will help you create a schedule that suits your family's needs and interests.

Pack Wisely: Bring plenty of snacks, toys, and entertainment for your children, especially if you plan to spend long hours traveling. Remember to also bring weather-appropriate clothing, sunscreen, and insect repellent.

Stay in Family-Friendly Accommodations: Look for accommodations that offer amenities such as play areas, kid-friendly menus, and babysitting services.

Take Breaks: Children get tired easily, and it's important to take breaks during your travels. Take breaks in parks or playgrounds, have a picnic, or simply relax in a café.

Take Advantage of Public Transportation: Geneva's public transportation system is efficient and reliable, and many attractions are easily accessible by bus or train. Children under the age of six travel for free on public transportation.

Visit the Geneva Botanical Gardens: The Geneva Botanical Gardens is a beautiful and educational attraction that is perfect for families. Children can explore the gardens, learn about different plant species, and participate in various activities.

Enjoy Lake Geneva: Lake Geneva is a beautiful and refreshing place to visit with children. Take a boat ride, enjoy a picnic, or simply relax on the shore while the kids splash around in the water.

Explore the Old Town: Geneva's Old Town is full of history and charm, with narrow streets and beautiful architecture. It's a great place to explore with children, and there are plenty of cafes and restaurants where you can take a break and refuel.

Tips for Traveling with Disabilities

Research Accessibility: Before your trip, research the accessibility of the attractions and accommodations you plan to visit. This will help you plan your itinerary and ensure that you have a comfortable and enjoyable trip.

Request Assistance: Many attractions and public transportation services offer assistance to visitors with disabilities. Don't hesitate to request assistance if you need it.

Consider Hiring a Guide: Hiring a guide who is familiar with the city's accessibility options can be helpful in navigating the city and making the most of your trip.

Use Public Transportation: Geneva's public transportation system is wheelchair accessible, and many buses and trams have ramps and designated seating for people with disabilities.

Be Prepared: Pack any necessary medication, equipment, or assistive devices that you may need during your trip. Ensure that you have all the necessary travel documents, such as a doctor's note, if required.

Visit Disability-Friendly Attractions: Geneva has many disability-friendly attractions such as the Red Cross and Red Crescent Museum, the Geneva Museum of Art and History, the Museum of International Committee of the Red Cross, Reformation Wall and the Parc des Bastions

Conclusion

Geneva is a city that truly lives up to its reputation as the "City of Peace." Its picturesque setting, rich history, and vibrant culture make it a must-visit destination for travelers of all interests. Whether you're interested in exploring its numerous museums and historical landmarks, indulging in its world-renowned culinary scene, or simply taking in the stunning views of Lake Geneva and the surrounding Alps, there is no shortage of things to see and do in this beautiful city.

As a first-time visitor, it can be overwhelming to plan your itinerary and make the most of your time in Geneva. However, with the help of this ultimate Geneva travel guide, you will be well-equipped to discover both the top attractions and hidden gems that the city has to offer.

From exploring the Old Town's charming cobblestone streets and historic buildings, to taking a scenic boat tour on Lake Geneva, to indulging in some of the world's finest chocolate and cheese, there is something for everyone in Geneva.

Whether you're a history buff, foodie, nature lover, or simply looking for a peaceful escape from the hustle and bustle of everyday life, Geneva is sure to delight and inspire you.

So what are you waiting for? Start planning your trip to Geneva today and discover all that this breathtaking city has to offer!

Encouragement Quotes

The world is a book, and you only read a page when you do not travel - Saint Augustine

The experience of traveling "leaves you speechless and then transforms you into a storyteller." - A. Ibn Battuta

The journey, not the destination, is important. - T.S. Eliot

You can only purchase travel to increase your wealth. — Anonymous

Prejudice, intolerance, and narrow-mindedness die when they are exposed to travel - Mark Twain

"Exploration pays off." - Aesop

Let's keep in mind that one teacher, one child, and one book have the power to transform the world - Malala Yousafzai

If you go far enough, you come to yourself - David Mitchell

Useful Websites and Resources

- Geneva Tourism - https://www.geneve.com/en/
- Lonely Planet - https://www.lonelyplanet.com/switzerland/geneva
- TripAdvisor - https://www.tripadvisor.com/Tourism-g188057-Geneva-Vacations.html
- Geneva.info - https://geneva.info/
- The Culture Trip - https://theculturetrip.com/europe/switzerland/articles/the-top-10-things-to-see-and-do-in-geneva/

Printed in Great Britain
by Amazon

22529388R00056